The Wolf in the Flower

James Dalton Byrd

Vabella Publishing
P.O. Box 1052
Carrollton, Georgia 30112

©Copyright 2025 by James Dalton Byrd

Manufactured in the United States of America

13-digit ISBN 979-8-89450-028-7

10 9 8 7 6 5 4 3 2 1

I would like to dedicate this book to
Dr. Arthur Seamans
who lit a fire in me and inspired me to write.

Contents

The Wolf in the Flower

I did not see the wolf
hiding in the flower;
although, my knowledge
    and my lore
told me it was there.

In a mushroom's quiet pose
lies the secret
of a cricket's song,
in words, so tiny and so ancient,
that were written
    long before their music
    rang into the night.
Wingbeats,
    heartbeats,
       and the pulsing
          of a tidal pool
            bind us all
              as one.

Look again at the flower.
Do you see the wolf?

Cajun Cookin'

Tonsil blastin' blast of
  good heat and
a gumbo made of whatever
    didn't make it across the road.
Savory dishes of anything
    Mother Nature provides.
Spices and love and filé
    with a healthy dose of
    cayenne and roux.
Mmm, mm, Cajun' cookin'.

Foreseen

As darkness prevails, gentle rains will fall.
Zephyrs will bring a slight reminder
    of winter's approach.
One day's surrender, cloaked in night…
      a velvet robe spangled with diamonds…
      carrying a colder warning.
        Fall's herald walks
        the vales and braes
        Scattering crystals across the heather
        before dawn smiles anew.

A Learning Disability

A learning disability is but one side of the coin...
you flip the coin and a new possibility occurs
each new attempt brings new strategies
and each new strategy encourages new attempts;
thus, we learn to work around our deficiencies
    and
in some universes there are more than two sides to a
coin
        maybe this is one of them
and we haven't discovered all the sides of all the
coins

                yet.

A Promise

The seed sleeps
    and waits
in fertile soil.

Rainstorms toss
electric fire
  and winds bend the trees.

Yet, after the storm
  with its fury spent,
  clear skies will prevail

and the seed
  becomes the flower.

Cupcake?

I am a father,
a son, a brother,
a grandfather, and a husband.
I have been a professional guitarist,
a frame carver, crane operator,
environmental technician, printer, and a commercial artist.
I have been a teacher of biology, chemistry, and physics.
I slogged through the hot rice fields of Vietnam,
seen an enemy die, heard his cry and carried that pain for years.
I have heard the wail of a freight and responded to its siren
song,
chasing after wheels that ended the journeys of so many.
Respect is something I have given and
something that I have earned... so,
don't call me cupcake.

Sunflower

With patient prayers
from a primal consciousness,
a sunflower turns.

Hope

Hope is a tomorrow word.
It doesn't have much power in the past.
It is a fragile word
too easily torn apart by
demons and ghosts of
what could have been done
      or
what wasn't said.
        Yet,
hope still returns.
  It may be a little ragged
after its encounters with
unforgiving memories
    and melancholy musings,
          but
                it still returns.

A Question

The mystery has been on the minds of many men.
A question unanswered and unasked.
A problem unmasked.
For one who seeks enlightenment
there are barriers due to decorum.
So, without seeming a creep...
the moral equivalent of dirt,
how do you read what is printed
on a woman's T-shirt?

The Old Lady and the Man

They moved in a different world.
The old lady and the man.
She always led him by the hand as they walked
through the park
and up the street.

Her kind eyes told their story
and she would touch his face
as she looked at him with such sweet sadness
for the dreams
that would not be.

The boy she had raised was hidden somewhere inside
himself
in a land she would never know.
She structured his life the best she could
as time plied its trade
on them both.

His head was always tilted slightly to the side as if
listening
to some little song.
The carefully parted hair, the ironed khakis and
neat plaid shirt...
her devotion.

I am glad, now, that we didn't make fun of them
As children sometimes do.
We just stood quietly when they passed by
through the park
and up the street.

A resolution

I, a flawed creature,
am not so inept as to
not understand
that any resolution
is a trap
        of my own making.
I hereby resolve
to make no resolutions.

Amoebae

What strange creature, by God
moves along by pseudopod?

Scanning its tiny land,
I fall deep into thought and...

Consider Amoebae
anthropomorphically...

we are inferior,
the blob is superior.

And how came this to pass?
You can't kick it in the ass.

Dawn

Spirits of morning,
rising from the mountain lake,
dance in the new light.

At a Play

Actors remove us from ourselves
        for a few moments.
They take us to places and
into lives we could not know without them.
We slip the confines of
        our identities…
and enter into other bodies
        and entities.
We experience the joys of others,
their pain, or their triumphs.
Much is given by the actors.
It is our task
to learn from it.

Ivy

I put the little ivy plant out to die.
It did not fare well in the window.
Placing it on a bench by the old wooden fence,
I thought it would enjoy fall's last sun
before winter ended its struggle.

The frosts came and exacted their toll
as plants around the ivy gave up their colors.
Leaves fell and winter came to claim its due.
Yet, small green leaves still peeked from the pot
beneath a hood of freezing white.

Winter surrendered to spring's hope
and plants rejoiced in the warming sun.
There was much activity for them to do.
They had to grow and show their glory again.
Amid it all, small green leaves still peeked from the pot.

They grew slowly and hung over the edge.
The pot disappeared beneath the green hope
of a living thing's desire to be what it is.
It fought back at the summer's heat
and withstood the dry time that came with it.

I marveled at this small green fighter.
That bench was to be where it met its fate,
but its fate was not what I expected.
It had become a place of resurrection.
A teaching place to school me in life's tenacity.

The cold returned and the sun lowered in the sky.
But, there was more than just a little bit of green.
The ivy's tendrils had spread on the top of the bench.
It was showing the world what it was to become
and it was prepared for the winter's fast.

It has now grown to cover much of the fence
and spread out a little on the ground.
It hangs there in quiet dignity, its leaves waving,
and it tells me, without reproach, it belongs here
and so, do I.

Devotion

A love song needs no words.
It needs no music.
The most beautiful love song
has a soft rhythm
that is shared by two hearts.

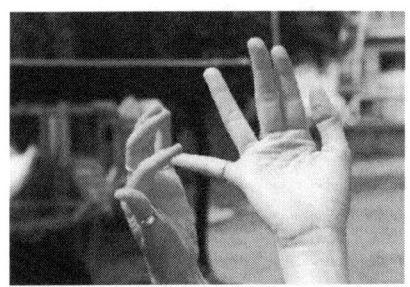

I Saw Her Hands

She was lying on a bench,
dappled with leaf shade and sun,
in a reverie of her own.
A table was hiding her
but I saw her hands.
Her hands danced in the air.
They became two swans
on an invisible pond.
Hands moving with grace and beauty,
touching my heart with
their dreamy movements.
The dance was guided
by a creative mind
whose beauty I appreciate
in a gentle friend.

Fort Worth

You will never be as glitzy as your sister, Dallas.
You are like a good-hearted, less sophisticated relative
that is a lot of fun to be around,
      but, by damn, that is your saving grace.

There is a lot more relaxation per mile in your streets and
you swirl, elegantly, in the eddies
created by the fast waters of go-get-'em Big D.
      but, by damn, that is your saving grace.

At one time you tried to shun your cow town image
now you glory in it ....and you would be more amused
than scandalized by an armadillo running through an
afternoon tea,
      but, by damn, that is your saving grace.

Old hotels and leathery smelling stores with creaking
floors
whisper stories of John Wesley Hardin and Pawnee Bill.
It is easier to hear the past in places where the past is not
buried
   so deeply....so completely...
      and, by damn, that is your saving grace.

You put up with us and are charitable to all the wanna-
be's and goat-ropers....
and, hopefully, you will forgive this ungrateful child of
Texas
for only now discovering such a good old friend,

      but, by damn, that is your saving grace.

Vespers

Little tree frogs sing
a chorus of tiny bells
at the end of day.

At Big Moose

Remember summer mornings?
Adirondack-cold lake?
And how icy water
returned youth?

Browning, Keats, Sandburg, and Frost
with coffee for breakfast.
The way to gut a deer...
Zen hunting.

We talked of old guys with beards
until we became them
and the words of old guys
became ours.

Now, just stay with me, Old Friend.
We still have a few miles
and a couple of beers
left in us.

Dolly Went Away

Dolly was vivacious.
She was full of life
and laughter.
She was also easy prey
To bouts of depression
and outbursts of anger.

Dolly went away.
No one said where.

When Dolly returned
she was not the same.
Her bright voice had lost its joyful edge.
She no longer engaged in quick banter.
She had become bland
without spice.

I asked Jerry about it.

He studied his shoes
    and cried.

Lights

Broken sky.
Dancing in water.
Nature's way of laughing.
Sunshine.

Ripples

An act of kindness to a lonely child
 is a like a drop of water
  falling into a still pond.
The ripples
 may not show a great change
  in the surface of the pond;
   but,
   none the less,
they still move through the water
  and affect it
   to its depths.

The Butcher's Blade

The butcher's blade was shrapnel on her leg.
Her small leg.
Fear in her mind playing games
with her eyes.
The bloody butcher didn't care,
nor was he concerned
that happenstance placed this small woman
on his merciless block.
A conflict she didn't understand
made jagged shards of metal
sing and moan in darkened skies
and one of those butcher's blades
found her.

Thoughts

A bright leaf floating
on the surface of a pond
hiding deeper thoughts.

Haven

It flows so easy
from our ancestors' memories.
To be inches away from rain
        and cold
yet remain dry,
    warm ...
a comfort appreciated
beyond the span of our years.
Smell the rain,
   smell the breath of the earth,
   feel the chill air on your face.
Commune with ancestors.
    Lore is the bread and
rain is the wine
   and remembrance
is passed on.

Bumps and Scrapes

Bumps and scrapes are
   like strangers
      who come out of nowhere
      to impact your life.
Some are kind, in a way,
   in that,
though they brought pain,
    some of the older ones
    become guardians
      of sweeter memories.
Memories, not of the pain
      but
of the people who cared.

Suncatchers

Goldfinches shining
in the early morning sun
sing to the new day.

Emily

Spring was in your face
   and the sun,
     the sun burst from your smile.
You were my favorite kind of human being…
a free spirit without malice.
 This sad old world is a little sadder now;
    but,
always richer
for having held your sweet soul within it.
May your next adventure hold promise for us all.

    Fly away, sweet dove.

Morning Light

Dawn slips into day…
a beauty always stirring.
The daystar rises.

Projection

When I was a child,
    seventy years or so ago,
my teacher would see me
staring out the window.
  "Stop daydreaming."
    she would say.
I don't think she understood
the art of time-travel
    and astral projection.
She did not understand that,
    as she spoke of distant places like Tibet,
      I was there…
        breathing the breath of great mountains,
        drinking glacial water,
        hearing the chants of the monks,
          and tying my prayers
            against the wind.

I am the virus,

I don't give a damn about
  your politics,
  your religion,
  your social strata,
  or your economic status.
To me, you are just
  a host…
  a piece of meat
  to infect.
I love your ignorance,
  your arrogance,
  your bigotry,
  your conceit,
  and your stupidity…
        for
those are the traits that allow me
  to thrive,
  produce progeny,
  to infect,
  to kill.
I fear your intelligence,
  your humility,
  your tolerance,
  your decency,
  and your wisdom.
Most of all
  I fear that which
  I can never know.
  I fear love.
  Love makes healers.

Summer's End

The last butterfly
leaving on its long journey
stops to say good-bye.

In the Glowing of Fall

I want to be with you when the red leaves fall,
when the frost returns and the high geese call.
When the spring has passed with its innocent ways
and memories now hold our warm, summer days.

I want to share a fire when stars sting the night
and the dark hills hide all else from our sight.
When, with soft tyranny, smoke demands our tears
and we remember other nights, fires, and years.

I want to hold your hands and warm them in mine
as I drink, with you, the last of life's sweet wine.
I want to be with you in the glowing of Fall,
when the frost is here and the last geese call.

James Dalton Byrd

At Winter's End

I want to be with you
as wind passes through the trees…
and the rain falls lightly
like tears onto the earth.

I want to be with you
when our work here is done…
and our hearts beat no more
for others to hear.

I want to be with you
as we pass through Death's gate…
into the light
of eternal peace.

I want to be with you
as forever becomes part of our existence…
and we live only
in others' memories.

I want to be with you
at winter's end…
When we walk on God's shore
hand in hand as the lovers we've always been.

Kathryn Grace Byrd

Mi Pequeño Amigo

A Monarch stops by
on its way to Mexico…
Vaya con Dios.

Requiem for a Robot

Little thing on a cold world.
Sent to explore.
Built to operate for a few months
but, plugging along
doing its work
for fifteen years.
It became a friend
teaching us.
We started thinking of it
as a living being.
We didn't realize
what it had become
until its last words…

"My battery is low and it is getting dark."

Screwm

A slow marinade of
mellow brew poured
over a good day's work.

A glass of red shared
with family and friends
on a special occasion.

A bit of single malt barley
and good-natured lies
with an old pal.

There are those who would
try to take these things away.
Well, screwm.

Song of the Butterfly

When a man is young and speaks no tongue
he hears the song of the butterfly.
But, when he grows up, his soul corrupt
from the reasons of how and why,
he still has the need but not the seed
that grows the song of the butterfly

Sweet Potato Parthenon

A farmer's need
to store a humble crop
    became
        an expression
of classic beauty.

Design...
    dictated by the necessity
of air circulating,
remaining cool,
        dry...
produced a structure
of perfect proportion.

The Bridge

When I was young,
I watched another young man
    being beaten while crossing a bridge.
    I was indifferent to his suffering.
It took a war,
    and the deaths of other young men
    similar to the man on the bridge,
  to show me the curses that lay hidden
        within tribal identity.
It took my years as a musician
    to recognize the talents of people
    like the man on the bridge.
It took the murders of those
  who spoke truth and
    stood against injustice.
    People who walked with
        that young man on the bridge.
I am no longer young…
    but maybe
      a little wiser, and
  I would like for that man
      to know
        that I have crossed the bridge.

The Fifth Man

There was Burton, Baldwin, Manny
    and me…
going out that night.
As shadows crawled over the rice paddies,
Burton, Baldwin, Manny, and I
    settled in and waited.
Then, there was that fifth guy
He was careless.
He was noisy…
not paying attention.
He wasn't carrying his rifle at the ready.
    And…
he wasn't wearing our uniform.

The fifth man came home with me.
Fifty-five years have passed.
    I still see his face.

Summer Song

A bluebird's soft call,
song of a new summer,
brings me peace again.

The Lady Taught Me to Sing

With an old wicker rocking chair
creaking out a loving rhythm
I heard the chariots swing low
as sleep came a-callin'.
"Mares eat oats and does eat oats"
in times of whimsy
And "Amazing Grace" when fever burned
and spirit's were fallin'.
"When we've been there ten thousand years…"
resting in God's home.
I know the sweetness of heaven.
That rocking chair was the closest thing.
All warm and safe was the child in my mother's
arms.
The sweet songs whispered true
as the lady taught me to sing.

The Season of Lights

The world has seen such madness before
when stress and fear hold sway over so many.
Then comes the season of lights
pushing back against a flood of darkness.
Tiny beacons of red, green, blue, and yellow
promising the best the human theater has to offer.

December 2022

You Are Beauty

You are the beauty of sunrise,
the beauty of the sea.
You are as the beauty of the night sky
because the atoms
of which all things are made
were born in stars.
You are made of star-stuff.
Never think ill of yourself
because, as God made the stars,
He made you
and you are the beauty
of God's love.

Sing, Wounded Soul

I cannot hold your cries,
they slip through my fingers.
I cannot take away your pain,
it lies so far beyond my reach.
I cannot dig out your sorrow,
its roots are too deep.
I cannot chase away your fears,
they hide and creep out later.
I can only tell you, you are loved.
So, sing, wounded soul…
your tears do not fall into emptiness.

The Spirits of Autumn

The leaves are woven
   into a colorful tapestry
      by the spirits of autumn.
         Sundown brings cold air, frost,
            and memories of campfires
               from when I was young.
                  Geese call from dark skies
                     and tell me of their loneliness.
                  I tell them I have friends,
                     near by... and far away.
                        But the geese ignore me
                           and keep on calling
                              and their cries follow them
                                 into the night.

Theology

I remember.
When I was very young,
God was a big friendly guy
who loved us all.
Then, as I grew older,
People began to tell me that
    I must fear God.
"God will get even with you!"
a preacher once told me.
"God will punish your children
if you are not right with God."
        What?
That sounds pretty petty to me.
The Creator of all that is
        is interested in getting even?
    With me?
I prefer the God of a five year old child.
I think God does, too.

There's a Hole in My Book

Dammit, there's a hole in my book.
    And,
            I like it.
I realized that all my favorite books
    have holes in them.
The holes were punched in my books
    by the authors!
A good writer places a hole
in the beginning of the story.
You fall into the hole
and you are trapped.

Thoughtwaves

Sing of the electric soul,
of atoms and ions,
of axon highways
veering through thoughts
and dreams
ideas and aspirations
hopes, horrors, and joys.
Neuron pathways changing,
bending, and careening
along thought roads
making new vistas
with each variation of route
blasting music and aromas
through mental tunnels
wherein the birth
of creativity and inspiration
are the graffiti
along the walls and
 the grittiness of the lower environs
gives way, falls aside,
and opens into petals
of belief and science
and art
all carried
on exactly the same,
minute electric impulse.

To share my life

It was a gift
given from the heart.
The promise made
within your eyes...
to share my life.

Whatever comes,
whatever will be,
will be a blessing
because I have you
to share my life.

Winter Vignette

All bundled up and chasing my breath,
I passed a house, blue in the grey light.
I waved at the child in the window.
She held vigil against the chill night
and gazed at the winter covering the hills.
Her cat brushed against her arm
and she absently scratched the cat's ear.
Freezing rains, weeping along the sill,
formed frozen tears to mourn the passing
of last summer's bright play.
The child turned and called to her father.
A moment later the door opened
and a good friend beckoned.
Amber light invaded winter's ice
promising hot soup and a warm smile.

A Southern Christmas

We don't have a lot of snow,
    if any at all,
like on pretty Christmas cards.
we don't hear sleigh bells ringing
or see chestnuts roasting.

Sometimes we decorate a pine tree
    or maybe a palmetto,
        or hang a few shiny things on...
            a cactus.

But there's really no difference,
    dear friends and family
        far and near,
it's the love we have for you
        that makes it all the same.

Y'all have a Merry Christmas, y'hear.

December 2015

55

Golden Palace

Last rays of the sun
transform the autumn forest.
A golden palace.

Pelican

Ungainly waddle-walker,
comical Stan Laurel of birds,
sailing unseen forces
just above the waves
in flight envied
by angels.

Writer's Block

The Muse thinks it's funny and slips away,
  dancing at the edge of awareness.
I chase it through nightmare-thick neurons
  running with little hope of success.
Doubt drags at sticky heels, not allowing
  Dame Fantasy to make her swift run.
And flat ideas skip across the mind
  seeking creative depth but finding none.
Where now, is my ability to pound
  elusive, raw words into poetry's mold.
I am trapped in here with only myself.
  The hammer lies silent, the furnace cold.

Silver

The moon pours silver
onto the stars in a pond...
and small frogs approve.

Memory's Door: A Journal

Memories written hold fast
after time fades what has passed.
Write then, traveler... of trails
through the dark north woods and vales.
Where bear and moose still roam
and ferns spring from fragrant loam.
Look far from the mountain peak.
Look for adventures to seek.
Behold the big waterfall.
Stand in Independence Hall.
Walk in sad Gettysburg streets,
and feel this great land's heartbeats.
and when you travel no more,
you have this book... Memory's Door

The Debt

A leaf is falling...
carrying its sustenance,
repaying its debt.

The Child I Am

As a child, I believed in a childlike world.
I saw magic in things adults considered foolish.
They stopped seeing the...
> mysteries of a spider's world
> > under a mailbox,
> and the treasures to be found
> > hiding behind old chairs.

Many lost the ability to see the wonder, and
beauty,
> of common things.

I have decided that, sometimes,
> it is better to remember the child,
> > and
> experience the joy of the child.

I will smile at people and say nice words to them.
I will thank kind people and try to be kind.
I'm gonna believe in Santa again.
Merry Christmas.

December 2024

Bang!

Ffffffffffffffffffffffffttt.

Sizzle.

pop?

"What time is it?" Time asked.
"I don't know," answered Chaos,
"Isn't that your job?"
"I just got here," Time said,
and pulled out his watch.
He squinted at it and he shook it.
"It's busted!" Time said.
Chaos winked and gave a nudge,
"Yeah, that's my job."

Time and Chaos sat
at the edge of it all
and laughed as they sang,
"Dust and rust, rust and dust.
Our best work is the death of work
and all that is built we grind to silt!
Dust and rust, rust and dust.
Our best work is dust and rust!"

They wiggled their toes in mysterious waters,
dashing galaxies and kicking stars.
Splashing light across the night
in such delight.
Worlds were smashed
in silent thunder
"Dust and rust!"
"Who cares, as long as it passes."

Then, God played a joke on Time and Chaos.
He made Dust breathe and think
and grab ideas from the darkest ink
and turn the rust to the Devil's drink
to make machines that
whoosh, bang, and clink

"'Dust thou wert', little one," said Chaos.
"'And dust thou art,' it is said," said Time"
'and dust thou wilt be again!'" laughed the both of them
as they danced through fields of stars.
They snapped their fingers and the machines did rust.
They thumbed their noses and gears clogged with dust.
But Dust began to dig and toil
because they made his temper boil
and then he found the hidden oil.
......and.....
whoosh, bang, and clink.
whoosh, bang, and clink.

Dust worked through the day and the night
to keep things a-runnin.
Time and Chaos worked through the night and the day
to break things down and wear them away.
　　　　whoosh,　bang,　and ...

"God, I'm tired," said Dust,
"I need some help."
　　　　　　　　　... clink.

"Hmmm," hmmmed God, "That I'll fix."
He took a little dust (the basic mix)
and added the light of stars to make it bewitchin',
and a little bit of Hell to make it be bitchin'
(just to keep things rollin')
"Now Dust," God said, "your help is here."
"This is She."

"She will do her best to manage Time.
And Chaos will have to sneak in when She's not lookin'.
Care and tenderness are her domain.
Pride is the best you can get from mechanical things.
She will bring love to your world of machines."

"Dust and rust!" Time and Chaos yet sang.
And they still raided Dust's little shop.
But they couldn't destroy as fast
the machines that
        whoosh, bang, and clink.

Time stumbled and hit his head, "Ow!"
Chaos slipped and ran into Time.
"What's that?" They yelled.
There was a tremor in creation.
A roar ripped through the universe
as a new little bit of Dust started to breathe and cry.

Dust and She now had a child
to carry on their work after they were gone.
They laughed at Time.
They poked Chaos with a stick.
They said, "You two have had your way but we are here to stay.
We have our work. We have our play.
We have our love and we'll just keep coming at you,
because that's what dust does best.

      whoosh, bang, and clink,
      whoosh, bang, and clink.

Immortality and Birdhouses

Careful measurements are made
and the saw cuts are true.
The entrance hole is drilled just the right size.
Passive ventilation is provided.

As I prepare places for tiny creatures
to protect and grow their young
I journey through memories and scenes
from a long and full life.

I played music and fought in war.
I loved and have been loved.
I taught children and learned from them.
I wrote poetry and made birdhouses.

It's not a massive undertaking,
the building of a birdhouse...
but it will be a, somewhat modest, monument
to me and my life.

When I am gone
and my ashes go to places I loved,
there will be no stone bearing my name.
There will be no structure to remember me.

There will be a birdhouse
that will last a few years to give me
a fleeting bit of immortality
and then it too, will be no more.

Catharsis of the Spirit

He was just a guy who continued in his existence without fanfare or glory. Most people didn't know he was there. Frank preferred it that way. In his youth he was sent to an unpopular war (he could not understand the concept of there being a popular war) but he went anyway. He became a medic and did his job as best he could; however, many times his best was not enough. The losses haunted Frank.

When he was hit by shrapnel from a mortar round, he spent a little time in a hospital near Saigon, then, he was awarded a medal and sent home to his family. His return was noted for a while. People lined up and waved little flags. Subsequently, people began to forget about what he had been through. They began to forget about Frank. That was fine with him.

New songs came and went, skirt lengths rose and fell, politicians bloviated and sent young people off to war, and Frank continued to suffer feelings of guilt. The memory of those he could not save haunted his sleep and he could not find rest. Eventually, Frank came to the conclusion that he must go to the wall. He did not want to go. He was afraid of what he knew would be waiting for him there.

Frank went to the wall. He had waited until it was dark to avoid the daytime crowd that was usually there. A few people were walking beside the wall and pausing for a bit before moving on. Some were making pencil rubbings on scraps of paper so they could take a name home. Some leaned against the wall. Some just stood and stared at a name etched in the granite.

His anguish grew as he drew near the polished, black granite. He could see people's reflections in the dark stone. Frank stopped and faced the wall. He saw there were more faces reflected in the stone than there were people looking at it. Young faces... faces that were becoming recognizable. The reflection of his own face, looking back from the wall, began to grow younger.

The fear and the guilt that had held him from this place for so many years rushed back into his heart, numbing his brain, muting the sounds of the city, and replacing them with the nocturnal songs of Asian insects and tree frogs. He wanted to run but the weariness of the years without peace held him. He looked down to see that which he had dreaded for so long. He looked down and saw his name on the wall.

The faces became those of boys he had known in Vietnam.

"We were *all* just boys." he whispered, "We were just boys."

The tears that had not relieved his pain for so long began to sting his eyes and blur his vision.

One of the faces came forward and said, "Its okay, Frank. It wasn't your fault. You did the best you could."

Frank realized he was now looking out from the wall at an older man who was finding peace at last.

If anyone had been looking at a particular section of the wall that night, if they had caught the light just right, they may have seen the ghost of an old man fade from sight as the reflection of a young man turned away with his friends and walked deeper into the black granite.

Nashville Vignettes

Nineteen-sixty-four was the year I turned twenty-one and, also, the year I turned my car onto the road that led from Texas to Nashville, Tennessee. Like so many before me, I was going to the city of music to find my fortune… or so I thought. I found part of my soul instead. The part of my soul that I didn't know was missing. It was being held by an old musician named "B.G.".

Gas Can Inspiration

Maybe there should have been some sort of warning, but there wasn't. Perhaps a little rattling or some bit of squealing would have let me know I'd better check the fan belt on my Renault. I had been careful about the oil level, the coolant, and the tire pressure, but the belt? Oh no, I wasn't careful about the belt. Somewhere along Interstate 40 I lost the fan belt. When the belt went, the electrical system shut down, and the motor stopped. I opened the engine compartment and saw the tattered remains of the fan belt looped over the air cleaner. After finding a piece of rope in the bonnet, I passed it around the pulleys to measure for the fan belt I would need.

It was the early 1960's and there were few cars on the road that late at night and Interstate 40, in Tennessee, boasts long distances between exits. I began walking back toward the last exit where I had seen a gas station. Since I did not know how far it was to the next exit, and since I didn't know if there would be a place to buy a fan belt there, I decided it would be my best bet to try hitching a ride back toward the west. After two hours and no luck catching a ride, I made it to a small, full service, gas station that was open twenty-four hours. Carrying my new fan belt and a waning belief in the goodness of humankind, I started following my thumb back to the car. Again, no one stopped to help me out.

I opened the engine compartment and found that the belt was the wrong size. My method of measurement was obviously not the most accurate of systems. I took the broken belt out of the engine compartment carried it and the oversized new belt back to the gas station. Again, no ride.

"What's the matter?" The service station attendant asked as I entered the door.

"Wrong size," I said and held up the broken belt, "so I brought the old one back with me."

"Let's take a look at it." He said.

He laid the belt out and searched for a number on it that would indicate the proper size.

"Ah! Here it is. This is the part number. I don't usually have much to do with them little foreign cars, but I'll see what I can find." He took the belt into the work bay and rummaged around in the shelves of tires, spare parts, and greasy tools. After a few minutes of half-hearted cursing and tire moving, the attendant returned with a new belt in his hand;

"Here you go."

"Do I owe you anything?" I said as I reached for my wallet. "Does it cost more?"

"No, it's the same price as the other one. We're even. I'm just sorry you had to walk all the way back for it."

"No worry, thanks." I said and left to go back to the Interstate. When I got to the highway I saw a couple of Semis roll by and I stopped as an idea hit me. I turned around and walked back to the station and through the door.

"Back so soon?" He asked.

"Let me buy a gas can."

"Sure, kid. Go ahead and fill it up and pay for it all at once." he said.

I reached for my wallet. "No, I don't want any gas in it. I just want the can."

Back out beside the Interstate, I held up the gas can as I put out my thumb to catch a ride. The first semi pulled over to give me a lift.

"Out of gas?" The trucker asked when I entered the cab.

"Nope, fan belt broke."

"Then why were you waving that gas can?"

"You wouldn't have stopped if I was just waving a fan belt around instead of this gas can, would you?"

"You're right, I wouldn't have stopped." he said.

Dave and I were talking with Willa about the possibility of picking up a few gigs as studio musicians.

"We'll need to join the union." Willa said.

"Yeah, and soon." Dave said and looked at me. "Can you pay your initiation fee and dues?"

"Yes."

"Well, good. We need to get this rollin' as soon as possible."

"No kiddin'." I agreed, "I have enough to cover a couple more months before it gets desperate."

Willa nodded and said, "If we head over to the 'Opry', we can catch Junior while he's on a break."

"Who's Junior?" I asked.

"He plays bass for Roy Acuff," Dave said and started toward the door, "and he's pretty high up in the union."

"How are we going to get in to see him?" I asked. "Do we have to buy tickets?

"No, we'll meet him backstage."

"How do we get backstage?"

Willa laughed and said, "We just walk in."

"They let you do that?"

"Yeah," Dave answered. He reached down and grabbed a case from the many instrument cases near the door. "You just have to have a guitar case in your hand and you can walk right in. I do it all the time."

I looked at Willa. "Yep, me, too." He said and picked up a banjo case.

"But the cases are empty." I pointed at the instruments lying on the bed.

"Don't make no difference." Willa laughed. "Just as long as it looks like you belong there, they won't ask no questions."

"Damn cool." I grabbed my guitar case and followed them out. "It's a lot lighter to carry this way."

"Yeah," Willa pointed at the instruments, "and any banjo worth a damn is heavy." We walked out of the aging hotel and onto the streets of Nashville. As we came near the rear entrance of the Ryman Auditorium, Willa noticed the instrument case that Dave was holding was not a guitar or a banjo case. It was the case that held his balalaika. A balalaika is a Russian instrument that has a neck similar to a guitar but the body is triangle shaped. The case looked like a guitar case until you got to that triangle part.

"What the Hell did you grab that case for?" Willa asked.

"Oh, shit. I thought I was getting a guitar case."

"Well," Willa looked at both of us and said, "you guys can walk back to the hotel if you want to, but I going in to see Junior."

"It's alright," Dave said, "I don't think anyone will notice it's not a bona fide instrument of country music."

We climbed the back stairs and walked into the open door leading to the backstage area. There were several performers standing around just inside the entrance.

"Hey, boy," one individual wearing a western-cut suit that was covered in sequined cacti and rhinestone guitars called out to Dave, "somebody done bit the ass-end off your guitar."

Dave thanked him for his observation, "It's a balalaika."

"A what?" the wearer of the colorful suit asked.

"A balalaika. It's a Russian instrument." Dave said.

"A Rooskie instrument? Are you one of them damn Commie bastards?"

"No, I just play a balalaika."

"Hey, Buford," the suit of lights called to his friend, a large, meaty individual with piggy eyes and a mandolin, "this here boy is a Commie."

"A Commie?" Buford's piggy eyes narrowed, becoming even more piggy, "You a spy?"

Dave looked at the hulking mandolin player and said, "If I was a spy, do you think I would be carrying a balalaika? I would be carrying a banjo or a guitar so I would blend in better."

"Maybe so, but all you Commie spies are mighty sneaky. We learned all about you when we used to have to crawl under our desks in case of A-bomb attacks."

"I used to have to crawl under my desk, too" I said.

The big guy with the mandolin turned and looked at me. "Y'all have desks in Russia, too?"

"We're not from Russia." I said and we hurried into the darkened backstage area before anyone else got into the conversation.

"Them guys is Russian spies." We could hear the singer in

77

the sequined suit telling a fellow who was holding a banjo.

Dave, Willa, and I walked toward the stage of the Grand Old Opry. When we got close to the front, I could see some performers singing on stage. Dave saw Junior and walked around a Bluegrass group waiting in the wings and motioned for Willa and me to follow.

"Junior." Dave called out as he approached him.

A tall man with a sad hound dog face turned and said, "Hi, Dave." His face began to crack, ancient stone wrinkles struggled to life, and Junior produced a smile.

"Don't worry, guys," Dave said, "He's younger than he looks and he's not going to keel over anytime soon." He laughed and shook Junior's hand.

"I could buy beer without showin' an ID when I was fourteen." he said and shook hands with Willa and me.

"This is Willa," Dave said then turned to me, "and this is Joe."

"Good to meet you boys. Dave here has been tellin' me about you." Junior looked toward the stage and then at his watch. "You guys need to join the union if you want to get some good payin' studio gigs."

"Yessir, that's right." I said.

"Well, I'll get the papers to you and we can get the ball rollin'. Right now, I have to go on stage and play for a while. Just wait here and when I'm through, I get them for you."

"Thanks." We chorused.

"Damn, Willa, I'm thirsty." I said, "Where're these folks

getting those cokes?"

"At the coke machine."

"Okay." I could hear Roy Acuff receiving applause when he and his band, including Junior, walked onto the stage.

"Where's the coke machine?"

"Come on," I'll show you." Willa took hold of my elbow and led me toward the stage.

We moved close to the curtain. The band started playing "The Great Speckled Bird" and the audience roared and applauded again.

"It's right there." Willa pointed to a Coke machine that was center-rear stage next to the curtain behind the performers.

"Whaaat?"

"Yeah, it's that one."

"I'm not going out there to buy a coke while they're playing."

"Why not?" Willa wrinkled his forehead.

"They're playing!"

"So?"

A man walked out from the other side of the stage. He looked at Roy Acuff and his band. Then he strode up to the Coke machine and plopped some coins into the slot. Grabbing the lever on the front of the machine, he pushed down and the machine rumbled, clanked, and churned until a Coke slid out the chute near the bottom. He then placed the shapely bottle into the opener and pried the bottle cap off. The Coke made a hissing sound and then bubbled a bit while he lifted it to his lips. He turned to walk off stage and waved at Junior. Junior nodded his head in recognition without missing a beat.

"Damn! That's bizarre." I said.

"If you want a Coke," Willa nodded toward the stage, "that's where you're gonna have to go."

"Oh well." I walked out into the bright lights of that great old auditorium and made my Nashville debut at the front of a Coke machine. The machine accepted my coins. I pushed the lever and the machine clanked and crunked until it birthed my Coke. I waved at junior on my way out and he waved back, again without missing a beat. When I got to the wings, I noticed that I hadn't opened my Coke. I returned to the bright lights and the Coke machine to open the bottle. Junior and a dobro player looked at me and laughed while I walked back off stage.

"Cool! Hey, Dave," I called out to him and some friends of his. "I can tell my mom and dad that I've been on stage at the Grand Old Opry." I waved my Coke at him.

"Yep," he laughed, "you sure can."

We stood with some other musicians and debated the merits of various guitars until Junior came from the stage as another act was introduced.

"Okay, come with me. I have the papers in my case." He said while walking to the gig bag in which he carried his bass.

"Thanks, Junior," Dave said when Junior handed him the forms, "we really appreciate this."

Dave handed Willa and me each a set of forms. "Fill them out as soon as possible and we'll get them back to Junior."

"I'll walk out with you." Junior put his bass into the bag and we all headed for the back door.

When we came near the door there were people waiting for us. The man in the sequined suit, Buford, and several others moved to block our way.

"What the hell are you boys doin'?" Junior asked.

Buford stepped forward. "They's Russian spies an' we're gonna beat 'em up a little bit." The others nodded their heads patriotically.

"What? I've known Dave here for years! He's no Russian spy."

"Well, we gonna beat 'em up anyway. Just to be sure." The group of bobble-heads backing Buford bobbled their heads.

"No, you aren't gonna 'beat 'em up a little bit'. Look, you want the union on your ass? I got a lot of friends here and you'll play hell trying to get a good paying gig if you give me or these guys any more of this 'spy' shit!"

"Okay, but we gonna keep an eye on 'em."

A Sense of Where You Are

I was playing guitar in a studio session where B.G., an old, blind ragtime musician was hired for the piano. We were discussing some arrangements we would be recording when the man setting up microphones called out to B.G.

"B.G. hit middle C for me."

"Okay." B.G. was facing away from the piano and reached behind him and, without feeling the keys to find his place, hit the note.

"Damn, B.G., how do you do that," the producer asked.

"I jus' know where I am."

The producer asked if I would give B.G. a ride home. He gave me directions and I was confident I would be okay. Actually, I hadn't been in Nashville long enough to really know my way around except for main roads. It didn't take me long to get lost. I was driving around, trying to find something familiar.

"I hate to tell you this, but I'm lost." Here I was trying to get a blind man home and I had no idea where I was.

"It's okay, boy, you just go about two more blocks and turn right. We'll be right where I want to be."

"We'll be at your house?"

"No, that's where my favorite barbecue place is. After I get some ribs, I'll tell you how to get to my place."

"I'm lost and you know where you are?"

"Two things, boy, I can smell the barbecue and… I jus' know

where I am."

It was a small apartment in a one story building that consisted of five units. The design was very basic. In a time before fractals became common knowledge, I observed a fractal building. The structure looked like the rusty-red bricks it was made of. Wanting to be sure he made it to his apartment, I got out of the car and started to walk him to his door.

"You don't need to follow me, boy, I know where I am."

"Yessir," I said, "but I was told to get you home and that's what I'm doing."

"Alright," he said, "now, you come on inside an' we'll have some coffee."

I didn't want to say anything, but this was the first time a black man had invited me into his house and I was a little hesitant. The spring on the screen door sang softly when he opened it. B.G. walked in and held the door open for me. It was one room with an area off to the side for a kitchen. The interior was made into an "L" shape by the enclosure that was the bathroom. He walked into his small kitchen area and put the bag of barbecue ribs in the refrigerator, then he felt around for the coffee pot while I stood in the door, trying to make up my mind.

"It's okay, boy, ain't none of it gonna rub off."

"What?"

"The color, boy, ain't none of it gonna rub off."

"I know that." I said. I felt relieved that he was blind and could not see me blushing, then I felt guilty because he was blind and could not see me blushing.

"Shit." I mumbled.

"What'd you say?"

"Nothing."

"Yeah, you did. You said shit. Get on in here and have some coffee with me."

"No, I jus…"

"You said 'shit'. Now I ain't deaf, boy, I'm blind and you said 'shit'. What's the matter? Did that damn dog shit on the floor?"

"No, sir. You got a dog?" I looked around and did not see any dog.

"Feeny!" B. G.'s sightless eyes looked up as if he could see something over my shoulder.

I turned to see what was there, forgetting for a moment he couldn't see. I was embarrassed again.

"Dammit, Feeny, where are you?" An old dog came crawling out from under the bed and waddled up to him.

"This man say you done shit on the floor, Feeny!"

"No sir, the dog didn't shit on the floor, Mr. Walden"

Who the Hell you talkin' to?" He yelled.

"I was talking to you, Mr. Walden."

"Boy, you call me B.G."

"Yessir."

"That way I know you talkin' to me and not my daddy."

"Is your daddy here, too?" I asked.

"Hell, no." He poured water into an old percolator and spooned coffee into the basket. "Look at me, boy, dirt is my little brother. My daddy done been dead a long time. God rest his soul."

"Yessir."

"Feeny, come here." he held out his hands and the dog wagged his tail and nuzzled them.

"Why'd you name him 'Feeny'?" I asked, trying to make conversation.

"I always wanted an Irish Setter."

I looked at the mutt and couldn't see much Irish Setter in him.

"I know what you're thinking'." he said.

"What?" The statement startled me a bit.

"You're thinking this ain't no Irish Setter, ain't you."

"Well, yessir."

"I didn't say he was an Irish Setter, I just said I always wanted one."

A Fine Thanksgiving

It was Thanksgiving Day and I was far away from my family, so I decided to drop in on Vince and Mariam. Vince, the bartender, had asked me to come and meet his wife. "Mariam is great with child" he would say with his chest puffed out. This was to be their first born and he was very proud of having participated in a biological event of such importance. Their apartment was in an old carriage house behind the Victorian monstrosity inhabited by so many of my friends.

"Come on in." I had not even knocked on the door when Vince swung it open and pulled me into their apartment.

"Hi, Vince. I was walking by and decided to say hello to you guys."

"Who is it, Vince?" A woman's voice drifted out from the kitchen.

"It's Joe. I told him to stop in some time and meet you... and the baby."

The woman's voice broke with laughter, "Well he can shake hands with me but not the baby just yet."

A pretty brunette came out of the kitchen and smiled at me. "You must be Joe."

"That I am, sweet lady," I said bowing slightly, "and I will wait to shake hands with the baby another day."

"Woman of the house," Vince boomed, "have we enough thanksgiving turkey to share with our guest?"

"I don't want to intrude, Vince, I just stopped by to see you for a few minutes. There seems to be a problem with one of the taps for the kegs and I was wondering if you could stop in later and help me with it."

"Of course you will stay." Mariam said, "We have plenty."

"Come and sit at the table." Vince pulled out a chair, "Want some coffee?"

"Why, yes, that would be fine, thank you."

Vince and I sat at the table and spoke of pretzels and beer and the need to do something about the window behind the bar.

"That damn window does nothing but allow a view of the starlings nesting on the building across the street." he said.

"Well, Vince, we can't tear that building down, so you'll have to do something with the window."

"I'd like to put a stained glass window in there but it would be too damned expensive."

"Vince, my major in college was art. If you'd like, I can adhere colored tissue wrapping to the window panes and paint scenes on them. That way the light can still come through and the starlings would be out of sight."

"Out of sight! Good idea. Get the stuff you need and we'll reimburse you."

"I'll start on it tomorrow."

Vince leaned back in his chair and directed his voice toward the kitchen. "Woman of the house, is the Thanksgiving turkey ready yet?"

"No, man of the house, not yet." Mariam answered. There was an aroma of good, basic food that came drifting out of the kitchen each time I heard the oven door open as she checked the progress of our Thanksgiving dinner.

I could not put a name to the smell of the food, but it was a mouth-watering scent none the less.

The cold air outside pushed a few snowflakes up against the window panes and then cleared them away just as fast. The warmth of the coffee and the small apartment snuggled into me and I found myself nodding of to sleep.

"Wake up, compadre," Vince's voice and his hand pounding on my shoulder brought me out of exhausted unconsciousness, "Our Thanksgiving turkey is ready."

He and I sat at the table and Mariam brought out the dinner. It consisted of eight hot dogs split and stuffed with cheddar cheese. These good people were as broke as I was and they still wanted to share... to celebrate their observance of this holiday with me. The warmth of the room increased as a new understanding of Thanksgiving grew in my heart.

Christmas With B.G.

The Christmas Holidays were coming and everyone but me lived close enough to make it home a few days to be with their families. The owner of the bar asked if I could run the business and, along with B.G., provide music. I had no problem with that and said B.G. and I would alternate sets each night. When that old man learned that I would be alone on Christmas, he invited me to stay over at his place with him and Feeny. Since all my friends were leaving Nashville to be with relatives, I was happy to have a friend to spend that time with.

Christmas night came and I was sitting in a comfortable chair in B.G.'s little apartment. We bought some ribs "to go" from his favorite barbecue shack and were feeling quite content. Later that night, while listening to Christmas carols on the radio, B.G. nodded off to sleep. I sat there that Christmas and watched the small fire in the coal-grate that was the only source of heat. Feeny came to me and laid his head in my lap so I could scratch his ears. The snow outside the window fell in soft, fat flakes and I felt great peace. The fire in the coal grate needed a little more coal and, after I had put a couple of chunks into the flames, I heard B.G. mumble in his sleep, "Happy Birthday, Jesus."

I'm Working on It

"I think I'm starting to understand, B.G."

"Understand what, boy?"

"How I was intolerant and didn't know it."

"What you mean 'intolerant'?"

"I was... uh, raised... uh, thinking nig... negroes were somewhat less... ah...."

"You mean you was a bigot?"

"No, I wasn't a bigot. I just..."

"You was 'intolerant' then?"

"I'm workin' on it, B.G., okay?"

"Okay, boy. Now, what was it you're starting to understand?"

"I am starting to understand the difficulties you guys run into in a society run by white people."

"You still far from it."

"Why do you say that?"

"You from Texas . Right?"

"Yessir, but that doesn't make me a bigot."

"I didn't say all people from Texas is bigots, I jus' asked if you from Texas. Don't jump on no conclusions, boy."

"Okay, I'm from Texas, so what difference does that make?"

"Well, you bein' from Texas, ain't you ever stood in the middle of a road that stretches outta sight?"

"Yessir."

"Now, I ain't been blind all my life and them lines on the

90

highway are far apart where you standin', right?"

"Yessir."

"An' far down the road they's all gettin' together?"

"Yessir."

"Well, boy, that's jus' an illusion. They's jus' as far apart down there as they is where you standin.'"

"Yessir."

"And that is the problem. You standing too far away to see that the distance between them lines is still there."

"Well, BG, I'll just have to keep walking down that road until I do understand."

"You gonna be walkin' a long time, boy."

"Yessir, but I would still try to understand."

"Why?"

"Because I would like to be your friend."

"Why?"

"Because you're a hell of a musician and entertainer and I could learn a lot from you."

"That's a shellfish attitude!" BG snorted.

"You meant 'selfish'?"

"Hell no! I said shellfish! You start that "learn-a-lot" shit with me and I'll CLAM UP!" BG laughed and his eyes sparkled as he looked away at something neither he nor I could see.

Goodbye, B.G.

It was around March when I received a letter from the Department of Defense telling me to report to Houston for a pre-induction physical. Dave and I drove to Texas and met our agent there to file a hardship deferral since we had just been signed to appear at the Playboy Club in Atlanta in April. We got the deferral and played the gig for two weeks. I was then informed that I would have to report for the physical in Houston. Since I had a little time, our agent, Bill Newkirk, signed us up for a concert in Houston. Not long after that, I reported for the pre-induction physical and was drafted into the Army. There was the usual exercise in how to accept exhaustion and frustration called "basic training" followed by more of the same labeled as "advanced individual training" for Infantry. My first assignment was with the "Old Guard" at Ft. Myer in Virginia. From there I was levied out to be sent to Vietnam. On my way home for my leave prior to being shipped out, I stopped off in Nashville to see a few friends and say goodbye.

"Vince, I'd like to see B.G. again."

"No problem, I'll stay with the baby and Mariam said she'd take you to his place on your way to the Greyhound station."

When we arrived, B.G. was sitting in front of his apartment in a metal chair.

"Is that you, boy? I heard you was drafted. You a big soldier boy now," he held out his hand to me, "I'll make a pot of coffee and we'll talk a while."

"Yessir, I'm in the Army and I'll be glad to have some coffee with you."

"Who's that with you?"

"It's Vince's wife, Mariam. She's giving me a ride to the bus station."

We sat for a while and talked of things important and frivolous and then it was time to go. I got up and put my hand on his shoulder.

"Goodbye, B.G., maybe I'll see you later."

He grabbed my hand, held it hard, and said, "You be careful, Joe."

Mariam took me to the Greyhound station. She walked with me to the bus.

"You know what, Mariam," I turned to her just before stepping up into the Greyhound, "that was the first time he actually said my name."

After a year in Vietnam I was honorably discharged. Dave told me there was a gig waiting for me at a jazz club in D.C. if I wanted it. I stopped in Nashville on my way to D.C.. It was then I learned that B.G. had passed on.

B.G. was an old rag-time pianist who was my friend a very long time ago. I loved that old man and I know that, right now, there's a beer joint on a back street in Heaven that has some great music rollin' out of it.

War Stories

My son-in-law, Rob Ethridge, and my grandson, Ty, asked me to write about some of my Vietnam experiences, so I thought I would include them here since I don't know if I'll have time to turn them into a larger work.

First, a little background information. I was no hero like our company commander, Captain Foley (Congressional Medal of Honor), or my friends Larry Cozart (Silver Star) and Chuck Dean (Broze Star), or any of a large number of other Wolfhounds who earned the title "hero", with or without, medals. I was just a musician who wanted to survive long enough to get back to my life and start playing again.

My MOS was 11-Bravo (infantry). I carried an M-14, E-2 modified, fully automatic rifle that fired 7.62 NATO. It had a straight-line stock, a pistol grip, forward hand grip, and swing-down bipod which, with two magazines taped back to back, weighed about twenty pounds. Although an automatic rifleman had to carry three times the ammo load of a rifleman, I doubled that because I never wanted to run low on ammo. In addition to the automatic rifle load, I normally carried two claymore mines, eight grenades, a large cratering charge, forty feet of rope (for going down into wells), a bayonet, an entrenching tool, machete, two canteens of water, a bottle of tabasco sauce, and a small chess set. After I melted down the E-2 one day I was given an M-16.

94

A Lesson Learned

It was time for me to go to the airport with a full load of soldiers and climb on a Boeing 707 and leave California. There was to be a few hours layover in Hawaii and another in the Philippines: so, I figured I would be able to get out, walk around a little, and have a few beers with my contemporaries. No such luck.

As a sergeant called out names, soldiers would be checked against a list and directed to the boarding stairs beside the airplane. When they came to my name, they directed me to stand a little behind them and wait. Eventually the sergeant called out "Zappa" and the last soldier boarded the plane. A large, black car pulled up next to us and a couple of guys wearing black suits got out and approached us. They looked at my orders and asked if I was right-handed or left-handed. I told them that I am right-handed and they told me to hold out my left hand. As soon as I did, one of them handcuffed a briefcase to my wrist. The other one handed me a belt with a 45 automatic in the holster.

"Do you know how to use this?" he asked.

"Yessir."

"Put this on," he said, "and be careful. The safety is on, there's a full magazine, and there's a round in the chamber. You are to stay with the plane. You may exit in order to stretch your legs, but do not leave the plane. If anyone starts to come at you, shoot them. The ground crews will be warned to stay far away from you."

"Sir, just curious, why me?"

"Because you have a top-secret clearance."

"What?" That was the first time I heard anything about having any kind of clearance. I never figured that one out. Probably it was just a clerical screw-up somewhere along the line.

"You will be sitting in the first seat and no one else."

Just fine, I thought, *Flight time and layovers would be about twenty-one hours. I'm not going to be able to talk to anyone or catch a beer at an airport bar.*

The flight was a normal flight except I could hear conversations all around me and I was rapidly sinking into boredom. We had two inflight light comedy movies to watch. *The Great Race* in which Peter Falk stole the show and *Why We are in Vietnam* which was not too funny and lacked any plot.

When we landed in Honolulu, everybody but me left the plane and hit the bars. My only fun was to walk around the plane and watch ground crew personnel move away from me when I walked toward them. I gave up on that entertainment and went back on board to allow them to do their jobs. That meant I was sitting there with nothing to do for about four hours. What fun.

We landed in The Philippines and, again, everybody but me left the plane and I terrorized the ground crew for a little bit. Then I went back on board. Did I say back on board? Maybe I should replace "board' with "bored". A few more hours and we were airborne again heading for Saigon.

A bit into the flight the captain came back to the passenger area and sat next to me.

"I know I'm probably not supposed to be doing this," he said, "but I thought you might want to talk to someone for a bit."

I thanked him and we had a wide-ranging conversation.

"I volunteered for this flight," he said, "because my son is in Vietnam."

"Army?'

"No, Air Force. As a matter of fact, my insurance runs out thirty miles offshore from Vietnam."

"Why?" I asked.

"Sometimes we get shot at if we come in too low. We have to fly into Saigon at a sixty-degree angle."

"Damn, you're intruding on Stuka* territory here. You gotta be kidding. Won't that tear the wings off?"

"Nope," he said, "these birds are pretty tough."

Sure enough, when we started to descend to Saigon that 707 went into a dive I was sure it wouldn't survive. After the plane landed and started to taxi toward the terminal, a sergeant stood near me and told everyone they would have to wait until I disembarked and turned the pistol and briefcase over to whomever I had to turn it over to. After the Vietnam version of the Black Car drove away, all the other soldiers, sailors, and airmen disembarked. When Zapa's name was finally called, we loaded into 2.5 ton trucks (Deuce and a Half) and were taken to the replacement depot at the American Airbase just outside Saigon at Tan Sanut, where, after a few days, we would be assigned to our units.

Now, I must explain a few things before continuing. If any of you readers are of high school age I have some advice for you. Gain every skill you can and pay attention in every class you take because you never know which one will wind up saving your bacon.

When I was in high school (the olden days according to some of you) I was advised to take Typing. Yes, Typing, it would be many years before Keyboarding came along. I didn't think I would need typing because I was going to be an artist; so, I didn't take Typing.

Okay, back to Vietnam. The third day I was in the replacement depot, I was ordered to report to a specific building for assignment. I went in and sat in the third seat in on the front roll. More men came in and filled the remaining chairs. A sergeant came in with a folder full of papers and stood behind a podium at the front. He placed an ink pad on the podium and put some rubber stamps next to it. The sergeant looked at the name tag on the guy in the first chair and shuffled through the papers before selecting one.

He selected a rubber stamp, slammed it down on the paper and handed it to the first guy and said, "First Infantry Division. Go down the street until you see the sign for First Div replacements."

The sergeant looked at the name tag on the second guy, shuffled the papers again and put one down on the podium. He slammed a rubber stamp down again and said, "First Cav. Go straight out the door until you see the sign for First Cav."

I was next. He looked at my name tag and shuffled his papers again until he came to mine. He stopped and read the paper a bit and looked at me again. He called another sergeant over and they read my paper again. One of them picked up a phone and talked to someone. He walked away a little and read something from the paper containing my orders.

"Okay, I'll ask him." the sergeant said to whoever was on the other end of his conversation. He looked at me and asked, "Can you type?"

"No, Sergeant." I said.

"Twenty-fifth Infantry Division." And the stamp slammed down on my paper.

If I had taken that little bit of advice about a typing class a few years earlier, I would have probably avoided being shot at so damned much. Oh well, I got a few stories out of it.

* The Stuka was a German dive-bomber in WWII that could pull out of a dive that would have ripped the wings off any other airplane.

How to Build a Worthless Bunker

We were always tired. That's the Army way. We were always told there would be time to rest and relax when we were back in the 25th Infantry base camp at Cu Chi. However, when we were in base we would still have to do all the maintenance on our gear, clean up the area, and do whatever somebody up the chain of command thought up. A good example was our bunker. When I arrived at Cu Chi my fellow "grunts" had already built the bunkers on our section of the perimeter. We had grenade sumps to allow grenades to roll down into a hole and explode without killing us. There was an area with bunks for our air mattresses and a small table and chairs for those not on watch. We had good fields of view out our firing ports and firing tables to lean on while shooting with shelves for ammo and grenades underneath. They were some very operational bunkers. The problem, of course, was that they were built by grunts and designed according to their needs.

I'm not complaining about building bunkers because there were times when something like a really big cobra would crawl in there and it was easier to blow the damned thing up and rebuild. However, some rebuilds were a just a waste of time to assuage some officer's ego.

Early on there were snipers that would come and take a shot at us occasionally. They weren't very good snipers and were more a nuisance than anything else. We would return fire when we found them and either chase them off or send them on to see whichever god they prayed to. The problems with our bunkers started when the number of pot shots began to diminish.

As the threat from snipers went down, the level of Brass (officers) visiting the line went up. It seemed like each time a higher rank Brass came he would order us to tear our bunker down and build a new one according to *his* specifications. Each time it would be less operational. Eventually we had a bunker that would take a direct hit from artillery but had no rest area, a grenade sump pointed in the wrong direction, and poor vision (almost no vision) out the firing ports. We had to sleep outside and, if shooting started, we would not be fighting from inside the bunker. Some of my friends were contemplating going into the village to make inquiries as to who among them is the poorest marksman so we could hire him to take a shot at us every once in a while... just to keep the level of Brass down.

Bad Day in a Rice Paddy

My platoon was supposed to be in base camp a few days we so could clean equipment and relax before going back out. I was an automatic rifleman carrying an M-14 E2. I liked that rifle. It was like pointing your finger and anything I pointed at got hit. An automatic rifleman was required to carry three times the ammo load of a rifleman. I never wanted to run out of ammo so I carried twice the load of an automatic rifleman. Well, that time to relax didn't happen, we were called out on an "Eagle Flight". Eagle Flight meant that someone was in trouble and a bunch of Hueys (Bell UH-1 Iroquois helicopters) were going to drop us into a hot zone to help them. A patrol had been ambushed and were in a bad way. By the time we got there they had been wiped out. We did a count and found that one man was missing. There were indications that he was wounded and taken prisoner.

The guy was just a private so we knew that he wouldn't be a prisoner for long. They would get what information they could from him, torture him a bit, and kill him. We knew that time was not on our side.

We came to a large rice paddy that had just been irrigated to about six inches in depth for the rice to be planted. There was a pile of dirt in the middle and that was it as for as any possible cover if somebody started shooting. My fire team was walking point for the platoon that day and we started across the field. Glasgow, I think it was Glasgow, and I were on point and when we got to the dirt pile, we found out that the enemy patrol had joined a company. We ascertained they were there because the whole damned tree line lit up with rifles firing at us. Our platoon was now outnumbered by about four to one.

Glasgow jumped toward the pile of dirt but that was too far away for me so I just sat down and started feeding magazines into the M-14 E2. The little bit of water in the paddy saved me from some embarrassment because I believe I pissed in my pants. I was pretty sure I was going to die. I had lots of rounds to jam through that E2 and that's just what I did. I fired so many times the stock started to flame. Our medic told me he thought my parents were going to get a nice medal. He said when he peeked over the rice berm there were so many bullets landing around me that it looked like I was sitting in a fountain. One bullet hit the edge of my helmet, I guess, and knocked it off my head. I got a tiny nick in my ear from a piece of the helmet or a bullet fragment. Glasgow yelled, "I'm hit!" Actually, when he jumped for the pile of dirt (and other stuff I won't mention) he jammed the barrel of his M-16 into the mud and when he fired it, it blew up and cut open his side. I handed him the E2 and told him to keep firing while I dragged him out of there. Our guys were finally able to lay down a withering fire on their positions and we called in an air strike on them. We figured their prisoner was probably already dead or wishing he was. The airstrike came in and tore up the woods where they were hiding. I have no idea how Glasgow and I got out of

103

there because anything that happened after I started dragging him out is now a blank.

The supply sergeant was pissed at me for losing my helmet, warping the barrel, and burning up the stock of the E2. They gave me an M-16 since they were phasing out the M-14's. I was glad it was after they fixed the M-16's jamming problems.

A Very Uncomfortable Walk

When walking rear guard, you need to face to the rear every time the platoon stops. Glasgow, Abraham, and I were rear guard on an eight-thousand-meter sweep one day. One time when we stopped, Glasgow and Abraham were on one side of the ruins of a farm house and I was on the other. Let me tell you at this point that Abraham was so damned afraid of getting killed that he would shower with his helmet on. He would be distracted by his fear so much that, sometimes, we had to remind him what he needed to do. In this case, Glasgow reminded him to let me know when the platoon moved out. Of course, he forgot to let me know. I thought we had been in one place too long and walked around the house to see what was happening. Nobody was there, that's what was happening. The platoon was out of sight and I had no idea which way they went. I did not want to be captured because a couple of guys from another battalion had been tortured and mutilated before they were killed. Nope, didn't want to do that, so I strapped a claymore mine under my shirt and put the detonator in my pocket. I passed through farmland and tree lines, being careful to keep an eye out for booby traps, mines, and punji pits until I came to a cemetery. The tombs and headstones in a Vietnamese cemetery can be quite large and extravagant sometimes so I took advantage of the cover they provided to pass through. About halfway through the cemetery, I stopped and crouched lower. I could hear someone moving on the other side of the tomb where I was. I slid forward

105

as quietly as I could and eased my rifle into position. About five feet away, on the other side of the tomb, a black face appeared. There weren't any black Vietnamese so I was quite relieved to see one of my buddies, a guy named Davis.

He looked at me with an expression of relief and said, "Byrd, am I glad to see you! I thought I was lost!"

"Davis," I said, "I hate to tell you this, but you still are."

At least there were two of us now and our chances of survival went up exponentially. We made it to a road that we knew went back toward the 25th Division base. A little further and we came up on some other American soldiers and a couple of officers from the first battalion of our regiment. When I returned to my company area, I looked toward the showers. I could see a helmet just over the shower wall, so I went over there and gave Abraham hell for leaving me out in the boonies to fend for myself.

Just Hanging Out

First, a little background, Vietnam basically had two seasons... hot and dusty, then, hot and muddy. The monsoons brought tremendous amounts of rain and some areas where we had to walk through dust would be covered chest in water a few months later.

We had completed an eight-thousand-meter sweep through rice fields and swamps during the monsoon season and were gathering in chopper groups to wait for Hueys to come in and pick us up. We were in a large open, area of waist-deep swamp with one line of Huey-loads already in position. As one string of Hueys started coming down for those guys, we started moving into positions for our Hueys to pick us up. While moving out in our chopper groups, a Viet Cong decided to take pot shots at us. We turned and returned fire. Then, all hell broke loose. A group of gunship Hueys came in between the chopper lines and opened fire on us. They thought we were the bad guys and started raking us with machine guns. Being in water, it was very difficult to move, and I saw a line of bullet splashes moving toward me. I don't know if the gunner's finger slipped off the trigger or what, but the bullets stopped on my left side and started again just to my right. The bullets went across Sgt. Hunter. A bullet hit the top of his bayonet, I think, and a fragment of the bullet (or bayonet) hit inside his right jaw and moved around to lodge behind his ear. He dropped his 12 gage shotgun and I grabbed his web gear and lifted him out of the water as we tried to move back to a rice berm. The gunships finally stopped shooting at us and we moved back in chopper groups for loading into the Hueys. Our chopper had its skids under the water near where Hunter dropped his shotgun. I didn't want to leave it out for some Cong to find so, as my group was climbing on board, I threw my weapon in the cabin and went under water. No one could see me so the Huey took off and the skid caught under my arm and I held on. Sometimes, when leaving a hot zone, the pilots would skim the trees before climbing to present less of a target... problem was, I was hanging off the bottom of the helicopter and he was heading for the trees. I managed to sling a leg over the skid and pull myself up a bit. It seemed an eternity before one of my buddies, Froggy, realized I was missing. He looked back at the landing zone to see if I was still there and saw me hanging on the skid. Several guys held his legs and web gear and he leaned out the side to grab my web gear. I grabbed his arm and web gear and they got me inside the chopper. The rice paddies, by this time, looked like postage stamps. When we returned to base camp we did our usual rainy season ritual of stripping down, lighting cigarettes, and burning leeches off each other. Just another day in Vietnam.

A few years later, my brother asked if I wanted to go sky-diving. I said, "Nope, I've done all that I want."

Really Cool

They said it wasn't malaria. It sure as hell felt like what I thought it would be if I had malaria. While we were in base camp, I woke up one night with fever and chills. It took me quite a while to crawl the few meters to the battalion aid station. The medics put me on a stretcher and started the paperwork to send me to the malaria ward at Bien Hoa... but it wasn't malaria. They told me later that I had been rambling on and on about how the C-rations should have menthol flavored meat balls so that they would taste cooler in the Vietnam heat. The next morning, I felt like maybe a water buffalo, or two, had been performing a version the can-can all over my body. Naturally, there was no room for me to sit in the cab of the deuce-and-a-half, so I rode in the bed on a load of loosely stacked water cans. By the time I got to the hospital at Bien Hoa, I had been thoroughly beaten up and was in no mood

For any clerk to give me any crap what so ever. The first one I saw at the admissions desk looked at all the dirt, grime, and sweat covering me and said that I smelled bad. At that point I had had it. I dusted off the Combat Infantryman patch on my shirt, pointed to it, and told him he would shit my toenails for a week if I didn't have a bed ASAP. He found me a place to lie down very quickly.

The rest of the doctors, nurses, and staff were a lot nicer than that first guy and treated me well. The bad thing about the treatment for malaria, which I didn't have, is that, if your fever went too high, some burly orderlies and a nurse would show up with a rubber cot and buckets of ice. No fun. After it was over and the fever was down we would ask the other patients to rate our performance. After one of my ice baths, the guy in the next bed said I had come up with some interesting combinations of ideas as to what those orderlies could do to each other.

One night I felt the fever coming on. I did not want that ice bath again, so, I decided to play it cool and not let the nurse know the fever was rising. Yep, I had it all figured out, I would behave as if everything was okay and I wasn't burning up with fever. Nope, they would not know my temperature was rising. Nope. No way.

The nurse was walking by and said, "Hey, Joe, how is it going?"

So, with all the subtlety I could muster, I yelled, "I DON'T HAVE ANY FEVER!"

The nurse just laughed and waved for the orderlies and the rubber cot.

Tennyson Would Have Been Proud

The company had been out a long time and action was such that we did not take our boots off lest we didn't have time to put them back on if a firefight kicked up. When we finally got to an area that was relatively safe, we were told new clothes would be brought out along with portable shower units *and a couple of fifty-five gallon drums full of iced down beer* (our battalion commander was the best). They said we were to keep our boots, weapons, and web gear; but, we would pile up our dirty clothes and they would be incinerated. We did as we were told and were all sitting around buck-ass naked, except for our weapons and web gear, waiting for our clothes and cold beer. Then a Viet Cong decided it would be fun to shoot at us a little bit. Any shooting meant the beer would not be landing. That wasn't going to happen. We all jumped up and ran across the field yelling and firing at the sniper with nothing but web gear on. That must have scared the hell out of that poor little VC because he disappeared. The officers told us later that there were reporters riding in the Huey with the beer. They were watching as we chased that VC away and it would probably be written up somewhere as The Charge of the Light Brigade.

Sources and Inspirations

A Good Man

Just watching a man comforting his family. I don't know his story, but I hope all turned out well for them.

A Learning Disability

My daughter, who teaches special needs children, had a learning disability herself and understands, very well, the needs of her students.

A Promise

After a hurricane, many things were destroyed, but some seeds I had planted prior to the storm sprouted and produced flowers.

A Question

I enjoy reading T-shirts; however, I always ask permission when reading a woman's T-shirt.

A Resolution

Ever notice how "New Year's" resolutions rarely make it past February?

A Southern Christmas

Thinking of my family and friends Now scattered in different parts of this country (and to other nations).

Amoebae
Watching a tiny, strange world under a microscope.

At a play
While watching a play directed by a friend, I realized how we can become immersed in the portrayals of the characters.

At Big Moose
Most times The Tamarack Writers met at The Glenmore Inn on Big Moose Lake. Some of my most memorable times were at Big Moose.

At Winter's End and **In the Glowing of Fall**
In 2005, I wrote *In the Glowing of Fall* to give my wife for Valentine's Day. Later, while in the Adirondacks, I came in from fishing, put my kayak away, and turned to see Kathy coming out of the camper. She was crying.

Typical husband, I thought, *Oh, crap, what have I done now?*

She said, "I just dreamed this" and handed me a slip of paper with words that had been hastily scribbled on it. It was *At Winter's End,* an answer to *In the Glowing of Fall* which I had written for her three years before. I was amazed. She had written papers in college for her teaching degree, but never wrote anything creative like a poem. It is the only poem she ever wrote and *she dreamed it.*

Bang!
One day, as I was walking in the halls of Central High School of Carroll County, I looked at my watch to check the time. The watch had stopped. Then this poem started taking form in my mind.

Bumps and Scrapes

Many years ago I was in a Catholic hospital. A seven-year-old kid with broken bones and fractures. Late one afternoon, a nun asked if there was anything I wanted. Having had lime Jello (my favorite) for lunch, I asked if I could have some more. In the evening, she returned with lime Jello for me. Years later my mother told me that the kitchen had been closed and the nun searched all over that hospital until she found a nurse on the night shift who had some lime Jello saved in a refrigerator for her night snack. She told the nun she would be glad to give me the Jello.

That nun and many nurses, physicians, and caretakers I have met inspired me to write this poem for them.

Cajun Cookin'

A bunch of Cajun cousins and a restaurant in Eufala, Alabama provided the inspiration for this one.

Cupcake?

Someone who did not know me called me "cupcake". I corrected him.

Dawn

Sitting quietly and drinking coffee beside an Adirondack lake in the early morning. The mists rising from the water moved slowly across the lake.

Devotion

Written for an old high school friend and his sweet wife.

114

Dolly Went Away

I had a friend who was sent away for therapy. She was never the same afterward. Still sweet and wonderful, but never the same.

Emily

Emily was my niece… a beautiful human being who left us too soon.

Foreseen

Internet Challenge: Revise the following passage so that it will appeal to your ideal audience:

> "Tonight, expect early showers, with temperatures in the mid to upper 40s. Clearing after midnight, with temperatures dropping, and frost possible in the valleys and on the upper hillsides toward morning."

Fort Worth

I lived in Dallas for a while before heading for Nashville chasing musician dreams. Many years later, I went to Fort Worth and found that I should have spent more time there earlier.

Golden Palace

Hiking in the Adirondack forest in autumn. Leaves of vivid red and yellow and orange captured the rays of the setting sun coming across the lake and lighting up the trees.

Haven

Those of you who have enjoyed winter camping understand this one. You know the feeling of being warm and comfortable just inches away from cold rain or snow. To gain a little recognition of what our ancestors endured.

Hope
Hope is a tenuous quality that must be held tightly.

I am the Virus
During the Covid pandemic I was appalled at the abysmal stupidity, callous selfishness, and disregard for human life displayed by people who had the power to do something but chose to lie and let people die instead. Then, there were so many physicians, nurses, and people who cared that stepped up and did the best they could amid the chaos produced by political sycophants and an inept president totally lacking veracity and compassion.

I Saw Her Hands
Amy is one of a group of dear friends who gather each year to read and critique our work.

Immortality and Birdhouses
Maybe Ozymandias, (Greek for Ramesses II) should have taken up birdhouses for all the permanence his great statue will eventually provide. No matter how grand a structure is built, it will eventually crumble to dust. In the realm of deep time, the Great Pyramid of Ramesses has as much significance as a microbe fart.

In the Glowing of Fall
See: **At Winter's End**.

Ivy

A small plant struggling to exist was an inspiration.

Lights

Just delighting in the beauty of water sparkling in sunlight.

Memory's Door: A Journal

Kathy and I took two nieces on a road trip north to see the Adirondacks and other special places. We gave them each a blank journal with this poem on the first page.

Mi Pequñeo Amigo

Again, I am amazed at the 3,000 mile migration of a species of Monarch Butterflies to the mountains of central Mexico. One lit on the porch rail infront of me about the time of migration and I wisheed it a good journey.

Morning Light

Rising early one time at Big Moose Lake, I sipped coffee and watched the light raise the curtain on a new day. Sometimes we forget that our sun *is* a star to some beings far, far away.

Pelican

Anyone who has witnessed the pelican's ability to glide, effortlessly, just above the waves for long distances understands .

Projection

I tried, as a teacher, to let my students daydream when I could. I understood what fertile ground is broken in a reverie.

117

Requiem for a Robot
Although the last message from the Mars rover, Opportunity, was a more technical message, I prefer one techie's poetic interpretation of the information.

Ripples
One of the rewards of teaching is having people approach you in a supermarket and tell you that you influenced their lives for the better. Sometimes you don't even realize how much a simple word, gesture, or action affects a child.

Screwm
A toast to prigs.

Silver
Out on Deer River Flow in my kayak one evening in spring. The Full Moon came up over DeBar Mountain and lit up the water and tree frogs were in full song.

Sing, Wounded Soul
This is a poem I read everywhere I am asked to read my work. When I was asked to read to the Vermont House of Representatives, I had several copies for anyone who wanted it. They ran out of the copies I provided them and asked if they could make more copies. I decided that anyone who wanted a copy of *Sing, Wounded Soul* should have one. You may make copies to give to anyone you know who is hurting. The poem was written when I was corresponding with a Russian poet. I noticed her poetry was becoming despondent. I could well understand that... her only child had died. One of her poems, *Lonely Soul*, was particularly worrying. I wrote *Sing Wounded Soul* for her. She responded with *Yes, I will sing again.*

Song of the Butterfly
When my first daughter was a baby, I noticed the times when it appeared she could hear, or see, something I couldn't.

Summer's End
Sometimes you can see little clouds moving in the sky when other clouds are still or moving slowly. They might be the butterflies on their migration to, or from, Mexico.

Summer Song
I love the soft call of the bluebird. It is one of the herald songs of spring.

Sun Catchers
Enjoying the beauty of tiny creatures.

Sunflower
I often marvel at how plants can achieve many of their functions.

Sweet Potato Parthenon
This little building on the right of Highway 27 going south from Carrollton, Georgia, has always been one of my favorite places. Its proportions are esthetically quite pleasing.

The Bridge
A personal journey and a tribute to a great man.

The Butcher's Blade
   One night in Vietnam, during a mortar attack, I could hear the shrapnel moving through the air. Sometimes it would produce a moaning/buzzing sound until it shattered a tree or hit the ground. Once, after having caught a piece of that shrapnel, I was in the aid station when they brought in a small woman who had been hit.

The Child I Am
   This Christmas was almost the first one in twenty-one years I did not write a Christmas poem. My cancer diagnosis got me down a bit. I decided that I am not going to let that take away the fun in my life and I am going to enjoy every day. So there.

The Debt
   I was watching a leaf fall in autumn. It reminded me of the cycle of things in nature. Nutrients in the leaf were returning to the soil.

The Fifth Man
   Some scars aren't visible.

The Lady Taught Me to Sing
   I was remembering some of the songs my mother would sing while rocking a child in that old chair. I think one of my nieces has it now.

The Old Lady and the Man
   His name was Patrick.

The Season of Lights

I try to write a Christmas poem each year. This time it wasn't easy.

The Spirits of Autumn

This poem came to me one cold night in late September as I was sitting beside a campfire in the Adirondacks. Kathy had to return to Georgia earlier in the month and many other campers had left so I was somewhat alone on Deer River Flow. Some geese passed overhead and their calls echoed across the lake.

The Wolf in the Flower.

I was looking at the word "flower" and realized it had "wolf" hiding in it. Then I remembered how DNA is shared by all living things. A Mushroom's cell walls contain chitin instead of cellulose to provide structure. It is the same as the chitin in an insect's exoskeleton on which the cricket produces its song. All living things share DNA information.

Theology

I remember a woman, Bea Allison I think, who ran the nursery in the church I grew up in. She would sit in a big rocking chair with arms full of babies, toddlers, and love. Somewhere along the line folks turned love into fear and that didn't sit well with me. The final straw was a preacher in Georgia saying that, if you are bad, God will get your children. That sounded petty and vindictive to me. Sometimes I think some people just miss the point.

There is a Hole in My Book

I think you know what I mean. Some books draw you in and you can't put them down. Some even call you back to read them again and again.

Thoughts

Have you ever watched something, such as a leaf floating in a pond, while staring past it deep in thought?

Thoughtwaves

I was thinking about how nerve impulses are all the same and different thoughts are made of different pathways through neurons.

To Share My Life

Some friends were getting married so I wrote this poem for them.

Vespers

In the evenings of early spring, tiny tree frogs sing their love songs. They sound like little bells in the darkness and soothe my soul when I hear them.

Winter Vignette

Walking in a neighborhood on a cold day.

Writer's Block

Okay, it happens to everybody. For a couple of months I couldn't write anything so I wrote this poem about writer's block.

Publisher Credits

At Winter's End
quillandparchment.com October 2006,
>*Words from the River* (Vabella Publishing) 2013
>*The Compass of the Magi* (Vabella Publishing) 2022

Bang
>*Bang* (Due West Publishing)   2007

Compass of the Magi
quillandparchment,com July 2014
>The *Compass of the Magi* (Vabella Publishing) 2022

In the Glowing of Fall
>*Words from the River* (Vabella Publishing) 2013
>The *Compass of the Magi* (Vabella Publishing) 2022

Sing, Wounded Soul
>*It is necessary to Live!* Dina Televitskaya (Borey Art Center) St Petersburg, Russia
>*Bang* (Due West Publishing) 2007
>*Words from the River* (Vabella Publishing) 2013
>*The Compass of the Magi* (Vabella Publishing) 2022

About the Author

James Dalton Byrd is a retired Science teacher (Biology, Chemistry, and, Physics). He taught the young people at Harralson County High school before moving on to teach at Mt Zion High School, Central High School, and Temple High School of Carroll County, Georgia.

Before teaching, he was a professional musician/entertainer for twenty years. He also served in Vietnam (A Co/HHQ, 2nd Btn, 27th Infantry Brigade 1966-1967).

Made in the USA
Columbia, SC
15 April 2025

56585019R00074